# Forever Triumphant

by F. J. Huegel

**DIMENSION BOOKS**
BETHANY FELLOWSHIP, INC.
Minneapolis, Minnesota 55438

ISBN 0-87123-155-7

Printed in the United States of America
by the Printing Division of Bethany Fellowship, Inc.
Minneapolis, Minnesota

*Affectionately Dedicated*
*to*
*all fellow Christians who have either*
*entered into the secret of the*
*Triumphant Life in Christ, or who*
*earnestly desire and eagerly seek*
*to do so*

*Now thanks be unto
God which always causeth
us to triumph in Christ,
and maketh manifest the
savour of his knowledge
by us in every place.*

*II Corinthians 2:14*

# CONTENTS

# Chapter I
## VICTORY — GOD'S STANDARD

It comes as a shock when one realizes that the Christian life, as for the most part it is being lived, falls far short of the divine standard. The status of unnumbered Christians is sub-normal. They are below par. They are not out-and-out sinners along with the worldling, for they have named the name of Jesus in true faith and are indeed members of His Church; but you talk to them about a life of perennial victory, about being more than conquerors, about a life "hid with Christ in God" in unbroken and joyous communion, and you will fail to get an understanding response. You may provoke an incredulous smile.

Yet no truth could be more apparent, however cursory one's study of the New Testament, than that the divine standard for the Christian is a steady stream, if I may so speak, of victory. "Now thanks be unto God who always causeth us to triumph in Christ, and maketh manifest the savour of his knowledge by us in every place" (II Cor. 2.14). You have here a completed circle embracing time and place—whenever or wherever; that is to say, come what may or when it may, be the temptation ever so great or the emergency ever so sudden, victory is ever and only God's order of the day.

It would be just as silly to make our faulty, up and down, now victorious, now defeated Christian experience with much of self and little of Christ, some of God but more of the world the standard, as it would to take faulty measures and incorrect scales, and give to these unreliable approximations to the ideal a universal application. Perhaps none of us have ever given a complete expression in daily life to all that God has for us as Christians and desires that we shall receive in Christ. Our little measure is one thing; God's universal and eternal standard is another. God's measure reads: Always triumphant, in every place the savour of His knowledge made manifest.

No, we are not going to build a system of Christian doctrine upon an isolated text. The wealth from which one may draw to substantiate this claim of victory for the Christian at home or abroad, at church or in the street, at work or at play, in sickness or in health, come what may, is so great that one gasps in awe before such riches. Let us marshal a few of the outstanding passages and promises before our mind's eye. It will prove an army with banners, an army which nothing can withstand. We will be overwhelmed with the weight of such evidence.

"But thanks be to God which giveth us the victory through our Lord Jesus Christ" (I Cor. 15:57). Here we have the same divine standard set up, only that here the emphasis is not upon time and place. It is not upon "no matter when or what or where." It is not upon the fact of victory, "come what may." It is upon the terms whereby victory is ours. It is upon the fact that victory is the gift of God through our Lord Jesus Christ. We shall not go into this now. The "how" of victory will be fully discussed in later chapters. It is simply the fact of victory as God's universal and eternal standard which now concerns us.

"This is the victory that overcometh the world, even our faith. Who is he that overcometh the world, but he that believeth that Jesus is the Son of God?" (I John 5:4, 5). Here John states in his own characteristic way what Paul affirms in I and II Corinthians. Now in the matter of victory, John was wont to stress the essential condition on the human side. That condition is faith. You have got to do your part, and your part is to believe. Then too, in this great affirmation in I John, we are made to realize that victory is not something the Christian moves toward after a long hard fight, as a possible prize. No. It is something he already possesses rather as a point of departure. Victory and faith are one and the same thing. You could no more separate them than you could separate light from the sun, or pain from sin. The faith of which John is speaking is the faith which identifies itself with its object. It is the faith of Mark 11:22 where the Greek suggests "the faith of God." Not, "have faith in God," as our versions have it, but rather, "the faith of God"; the faith which God, possessing the heart, inspires. But more of this, too, later. We are for the present, simply establishing the fact of victory as God's eternal and universal standard.

" . . . they which receive abundance of grace and of the gift of righteousness shall reign in life by one, Jesus Christ" (Rom. 5:17). Here Paul traces the fact of sin and defeat and death as the result, in the final analysis, of Adam's transgression. By one man's offence death reigned. We belong to a fallen race, and as such, sinners stemming from Adam, we all die. By one man's disobedience many were made sinners, so by the obedience of one shall many be made righteous. The argument is that if we have been baptized into Christ's body by the eternal Spirit, our life no longer stems from Adam but from Christ, the Second Federal Head of the race, in whom we reign. We have been made kings and priests unto God through

Christ. Therefore we reign. Kings by virtue of their kingship reign.

We come now to what is the strongest statement in the New Testament regarding the fact of a perennial victory on the part of the Christian. It is Paul's defiant, triumphant cry in the face of every possible contingency, every conceivable trial or temptation, any and every emergency that might arise. He seems to challenge every force of the entire universe. He laughs at death, defies principalities and powers, hurls the gauntlet at things present and things to come; though he be accounted a sheep for the slaughter and be killed all the day long, yet victory shall be his. Neither tribulation nor distress nor persecution nor famine nor nakedness nor peril nor sword shall separate him from the love of Christ. There is no creature that shall separate him from the love of God which is in Christ Jesus the Lord. Not only will he conquer, come what may; he will be more than conqueror. When David slew Goliath with his sling and a stone, he ran to the fallen foe, poised himself upon his dead body and, drawing the giant's sword from its sheath, beheaded Israel's great enemy at a stroke. He was more than conqueror. "Nay, in all these things," cries Paul, intoxicated as it were with the life of God, "we are more than conquerors through him that loved us" (Rom. 8:37).

It is not victory now with clenched fists

and set jaw. It is victory swallowed up in praise. It is victory in the midst of ten thousand hallelujahs. It is victory surcharged with holy laughter. It is victory so assured and so complete and so final that all sense of uncertainty in the midst of the storm is lost. It is as when the tide comes in and sweeps everything before it. It is as when the sun rises dispelling the night and filling every nook and corner with golden shafts of sunlight. When Lazarus arose at the call of his Master, the command was to set him free from every trace of the grave and its clothes. The Saviour would have his movements be free and easy and unhampered. It was resurrection—plus. Ours, says Paul, is victory—plus. Ah, but what a "plus" does the apostle present!

We are not limited to direct, unmistakable affirmations such as these we have just considered. Victory, such as Paul describes in Romans 8, is hinted at in the gospel narrative of the Redeemer's public ministry. The lad's lunch, in the miracle of the loaves and fishes, in Jesus' blessed hands, feeds five thousand with twelve baskets full of crumbs to cap the climax. The prodigal of the parable is not only forgiven, he is robed as a prince, bejewelled as a favorite son, feasted as an honored guest whose sweet and joyous coming had long been anticipated with deep longings and infinite delight. When the disciples' ship, in peril because of the angry sea whipped up to high fury by a sudden storm, receives the Christ of God, He does not only still the wind and waves. No! The ship immediately arrives at its destination on the other shore. When the nets were filled miraculously by the Master's word of command that they should be cast on the right side of the ship, the haul brought in 153. One hundred represents the hundredfold fruit of the parable; fifty stands in vital relation with Pentecost with its flood-tide of divine blessing; and three, the glory and power of the Triune God—Father, Son and Holy Spirit. No, it must be "more than conquerors," for when God gives, it must be in keeping with the immeasurable generosity that characterizes the Father of Lights from whom cometh every good and perfect gift.

You have the same thought in the Redeemer's great utterance which aroused such a storm of protest and controversy on the part of the Jews. They said they were free, but Jesus said they were in bondage to sin. He said they were of their father, the Devil. But there was hope if they would but turn in faith to their Saviour and Lord. "If the Son," he bids them understand, "therefore shall make you free, ye shall be free indeed." Not only free, but *free indeed.*

"Grace and peace be multiplied unto you . . . " When God gives, it is always in a multiplied fashion, something akin to the unnumbered millions of shining worlds in the boundless firmament of Heaven. Multiplied " . . . through the knowledge of God and of Jesus our Lord, According as his divine power hath given unto us all things that pertain unto life and godliness, through the knowledge of him that hath called us to glory and virtue: Whereby are given unto us exceeding great and precious promises: that by these ye might be partakers of the divine nature, having escaped the corruption that is in the world through lust" (II Peter 1:2-4).

"For sin shall not have dominion over you: for ye are not under the law, but under grace" (Rom. 6:14).

"My grace is sufficient for thee: for my strength is made perfect in weakness" ( Ii Cor. 12:9).

## Chapter II

## VICTORY IS ALREADY OURS

For those who, conscious of their need, are seeking and would enter the way of perennial victory, it will be a great help to realize that they are not seeking something which they do not already have. That is to say, if they have named the name of Jesus in true faith and have surrendered to Him, crowning Him Lord of their lives, as Christians they have been made kings and priests unto God (Rev. 1:6), and as such they have a right to reign. If they fail to reign, they are simply not exercising their rights.

"This is the victory that overcometh the world, even our faith." The victorious life is not something exotic added to the Christian life. It is not an attainment of a few advanced souls who, after much effort and struggle, have scaled the heights and finally arrived. It is not something which a privileged upper-strata of Christians achieve because, after much searching and no little self-sacrifice, they experienced what others may not have.

It cannot be too earnestly stressed that

all Christians come into the same glorious inheritance. They have received Christ, and all things are theirs for they are Christ's. In Him they are complete. With Him they have been raised up, and with Him they have been made to sit together in heavenly places (Eph. 2:5,6). In Him they died unto sin and were made alive unto God (Rom. 6:11). Christ has been made unto them, of God, wisdom, righteousness, sanctification and redemption (I Cor. 1:30). These things cannot, in a sense, be made more truly theirs than they already are. When God gives us Christ, His holy Son, to be our life, and this unspeakable gift is for all who will receive it by faith acknowledging themselves lost sinners in need of the gift; He does not do so with reservations. The whole gift is ours, not simply a part. We receive the whole Christ, if I may so speak. We do not receive justification without sanctification. We are not brought into Christ piecemeal. Paul, in a sense, had no more of Christ than the poor drunkard who only yesterday in some mission hall heard the Gospel, repented, believed, received Christ as his Saviour, and was born again.

That is to say, there is no difference in the judicial standing of Christians before God. By their judicial standing, I mean the position God says is theirs by virtue of the fact that they have received His wondrous gift which is Christ and are found in Him. He says that their position and judicial standing is the very same as that of His Son, Jesus, whose identification with humanity was so real and of such an absolute nature that what befell Him as Son of Man, befell Him as Representative Man and therefore, befell all who are united to Him by faith. He was crucified, therefore man was crucified (our old man was crucified with Christ, Rom. 6:6). He died, therefore man died (" . . . ye are dead," Col. 3:3). He was buried, therefore man was buried (" . . . we are buried with him . . . into death," Rom. 6:4). He was raised up, man is raised up ("God . . . hath quickened us together with Christ . . . and hath raised us up together," Eph. 2:5, 6). He ascended, man ascended (". . . and made us sit together in heavenly places in Christ Jesus," Eph. 2:6). This is the believer's judicial position before God—his by an inalienable right; a right which, in a sense, is no different than that of Christ's Himself. A right which is no different because Christ and believers are one. "For he that is joined unto the Lord is one spirit" (I Cor. 6:17).

The trouble lies in the fact that not all believers realize what their judicial standing is in Christ. They are not possessing their possessions. They are not exercising their rights. They are not cashing their checks. The deposit of spiritual riches is in Christ at the believer's disposal in the bank of Heaven. They are not actuated by a bold faith which, refusing to take into account the unworthiness of the creature, casts itself upon the mercy of God in Christ and makes copious demands upon the bank of Heaven. They are wont to measure their moral and spiritual capacity by their own ability and effort, giving Christ a place, of course, but yet a scanty one. They have not yet learned to say with Paul, "I can do all things through Christ which strengtheneth me." They move too much in the realm of the natural. They have not realized that the natural is of no avail in this great conflict with evil. They have not fully grasped the meaning of the Saviour's Word where He says that the flesh profiteth nothing. They have not yet stood where Paul stood when he cried, "I know that in me (that is, in my flesh), dwelleth no good thing." They have not realized that it is their *good* "self" not yet denied which causes them to stumble. They are willing for their *bad* "self" to be crucified, not aware of the fact that the *good* "self" is just as mischievous, for it is still "self," and victory cannot be ours until all of "self" has been assigned to the Cross according to Romans 6.

The Christian, I repeat, who hungers and thirsts after righteousness, the righteousness of a perennial victory, full orbed, the more-than-conqueror type, is not seeking something that is not already his. In a sense God cannot make it more his than it already is. On the divine side it is a consummated thing. We get nowhere by looking at ourselves. God expects nothing of self but that it be crucified, which judicially it already is. We are not called upon as Christians to die to sin; but to recognize the fact that we have died to sin in the death of Him who, on Calvary's cross, put an end to the *old* creation, that in the power of His resurrection He might bring forth the *new*. Our old man *was* crucified with Christ, and in view of this fact we *reckon* (Rom. 6:11) ourselves dead to sin and alive unto God. The reckoning does not produce the fact; it simply springs from the fact.

Victory such as was described in Chapter I where we speak of it as God's standard ("thanks be to God who always causeth us to triumph ...") appears to be altogether unattainable for unnumbered Christians, a goal never to be reached here upon earth however great the longings for such a thing might be, or however earnestly one might strive to achieve such a position, for the very simple reason that they are not willing to believe what God says about the matter nor to do what He says must be done. How can they reckon themselves dead to sin and alive unto God according to Romans 6:11 (the Christian basis of a victorious position) when it simply is not yet a fact? They feel that they must be honest. To state such a thing would be a lie. How can they reckon themselves dead to sin and alive unto God when it seems as though every atom of their being still responds to sin, when the world still seems to master them, and the devil, in many respects, is still king.

But they are wrong. God does not ask them to affirm something which they can believe to be true because they feel it and see it. It is not a fact in themselves. It is a fact in the eternal council of God. It is a fact in the divine economy of redemption. It is a fact in the consummation wrought by the Son of God on Calvary's Cross. It is as true as its twin fact; namely, that Christ the Lord bore our sins in His body on the Cross. Feeling this latter does not make it a fact nor does believing it. It is a fact because, when the blessed Redeemer died the shameful death of a slave and a criminal of Golgotha's cursed Tree, God tells us in His holy Word (and the whole Bible centers in this fact and is as the chorus of a million voices resonant with its praise) that it was to put away the sin of the world. When the sinner believes and is saved he does not create the fact, he simply rests in the fact established since the foundation of the world when, as we read in Revelation, the Lamb of God was slain. Calvary was the visible expression of a fact already established by the determinate counsel and foreknowledge of God.

So it is with this twin-fact of the Cross so insistently proclaimed in all of Paul's Epistles. "Our old man was crucified with Christ." "Ye are dead and your life is hid with Christ in God." "I am crucified with Christ: nevertheless I live; yet not I, but Christ liveth in me . . ." We are told that it was a fact when on the Cross the Saviour cried with a loud voice, "It is finished." Not only was guilt dealt with; sin as a principle was condemned (see Rom. 8:3). The sin principle in you and me was crucified. You get nowhere in this question of victory until you believe it. You do not try to deceive yourself into believing you are dead to sin and alive unto God, when experience says something quite different. You are asked to reckon yourself dead to sin through Christ, because God says He dealt with the sin-principle that is in you (our old man was crucified) when the Redeemer died on Calvary's Cross. Victory is already yours if you are a Christian, but you must accept it in God's way and according to His terms.

## Chapter III

## THE SAVIOUR SPEAKS TO
## THE OVERCOMER

When we turn to the book of Revelation where the Saviour speaks to His Church from the throne, we are given a wondrous confirmation of the need and possibility of victory as the divine standard for the Christian. Jesus, the Lord, had promised to appear to John, the Apostle, who would "tarry till I [the Lord] come"(John 21:22). It was many years later on the Isle of Patmos where the exiled apostle was suffering for "the testimony of Jesus Christ," that the Saviour appeared to the beloved disciple, now grown old in the service of his King, and commanded him to write the things which had been revealed to him. The Saviour had a message to the churches of Asia; seven, the perfect number, that it might be understood that He was really addressing all. There can be no doubt about the fact that, though the messages were to the seven churches of Asia, the Redeemer was speaking to all, for these were typical churches chosen because they were representative of conditions that have ever prevailed wherever the Gospel has been preached and the Church established. To prove that it is so, the Lord, Head of the Church, closes each letter with the words: "He that hath an ear, let him hear what the Spirit saith unto the churches." Yet, it is indeed the Saviour speaking from the throne to the Universal Church—churches of all ages in all lands. It is the resurrected, ascended Christ, who speaks to His own, those who, down the centuries, were to make up His body, the Church.

Now what interests us in all this is the astounding fact that the Saviour, as He reveals His Word to John and through John to the churches, closes each letter with a promise. The promises are of a varied nature beginning with an offer of the privilege to eat of the tree of life and closing with the overwhelming possibility of a participation of the very throne of God. Such riches and glories and blessings are marshalled before the believer as to leave him breathless. He fain would fall at the Saviour's feet as dead, even as occurred with the apostle himself, for it is more than flesh can bear. However, the promises all have one thing in common. They are all made payable, so to speak, to the same person. They can be claimed only by one who has learned the secret of victory. None by overcomers can enter here. In offering such unfathomable wealth and glory, the Redeemer only takes into account one type of Christian. The rest are not taken into consideration. It is amazing, but the facts are before anyone who will look into these seven letters to the churches of Asia as recorded in chapters two and three of Revelation.

It is "to him that overcometh" that the key to the riches of Heaven is given. It is at the feet of "him that overcometh" that the glories of the Kingdom are committed. It is "to him that overcometh" that the very throne itself is promised. There is no measuring the significance of this fact.

Let us run down the list. To the church at Ephesus it is stated, "To him that overcometh will I give to eat of the tree of life, which is in the midst of the paradise of God." To Christians at Smyrna the promise is given that "he that overcometh shall not be hurt of the second death." Believers at Pergamos are told that "to him that overcometh" the Saviour will give "to eat of the hidden manna, and will give him a white stone, and in the stone a new name written, which no man knoweth saving he that receiveth it." To the church at Thyatira the Spirit speaks, saying: "And he that overcometh, and keepeth my works unto the end, to him will I give power over the nations: And he shall rule them with a rod of iron; as the vessels of a potter shall they be broken to shivers: even as I received of my Father. And I will give him the morning star." To the faithful at Sardis the promise is given: "He that overcometh, the same shall be clothed in white raiment; and I will not blot out his name out of the book of life, but I will confess his name before my Father, and before his angels." The Philadelphia folk hear the Master say: "Him that overcometh I will make a pillar in the temple of my God, and he shall go no more out: and I will write upon him the name of my God, and the name of the city of my God, which is new Jerusalem, which cometh down out of heaven from my God: and I will write upon him my new name." Finally, and this is the most stupendous of the series, perhaps the most amazing promise in all the Scriptures, comes the statement made to the Laodicean church: "To him that overcometh will I grant to sit with me in my throne, even as I also overcame and am set down with my Father in his throne" (Rev. 3:21).

This is not all, however, The same voice is heard in Chapter 21 where the Saviour, in accordance with what has been said of the universality of these messages and their promises, speaks to the whole Church saying, "He that overcometh shall inherit all things; and I will be his God, and he shall be my son." If the weight of the universe were brought to bear upon the need of victory, the underlining could not be more emphatic. Were all the angels of Heaven and all the preachers of earth to cry out and say, "Christians must overcome; they must be more than conquerors," the matter could not be brought to a sharper focus or be more earnestly pressed upon the attention of believers.

It, no doubt, will come as a terrific shock to many; namely, the discovery that God does not seem to take into account any type of Christians save those who overcome. At least such is the case in these marvelous epistles, which, as we have noted, cannot be limited to the seven churches of Asia. The indications of their universal scope could not be stronger. "He that overcometh shall inherit all things; and I will be his God, and he shall be my son." In this last promise there is no church mentioned. The Saviour is speaking to all, and the ever-recurring refrain with which each of the seven epistles closes: "He that hath an ear, let him hear what the Spirit saith unto the churches," should suffice to establish the universal scope of these promises.

The thought naturally comes, however— why does the Master sound with such force this note in Revelation? It is not sounded in the gospels. The note there seems to be quite different. The emphasis is on faith. No other requirement is made. It was sufficient to release the bounty of Heaven. "According to your faith be it unto you." "Believe ye that I am able to do this?" "Thy faith hath saved thee, go in peace." "O thou of little faith, wherefore didst thou doubt?" "He could there do no mighty work . . . because of their unbelief." What shall we do, that we might work the works of God? Jesus answered and said unto them, "This is the work of God, that ye believe on him whom he hath sent." "He that believeth on me . . . out of his 'innermost being' shall flow rivers of living water." "I am the bread of life: he that cometh to me shall never hunger; and he that believeth on me shall never thirst." It is thus that the Saviour speaks in the gospels. How then shall we account for this change in tone and emphasis as they appear in the book of Revelation? Here the Saviour speaks from the throne and demands victory as the condition on the human side in order to receive the wondrous blessings He has to bestow.

The answer is found, as one would expect, in the Scriptures and it is very clear and unequivocal. There is no contradiction or want of consistency. The picture is perfectly harmonious. There is nothing jarring or ill-proportioned in the relation of colors. The blending is perfect.

We turn to John's First Epistle, the fifth chapter, where we have a solution of the problem that is absolutely satisfactory. "Who is he," asks the apostle, "that overcometh the world, but he that believeth that Jesus is the Son of God?" "Whatsoever is born of God overcometh the world: and this is the victory that overcometh the world, even our faith." In other words, there is no problem. We do not have two gospels, but only one. The Saviour does not ask for one thing in the four gospels and for another in the book of Revelation. It is the same voice, the same Gospel, the same blessed Redeemer. The difference depends on the way you view things. You can look at a shield from one side or from the other. What you see will be quite different, but it is still the same shield. The "shield of faith" may be viewed from different angles, but it is still the same shield. In Revelation the Saviour tells us, in effect, that faith and victory are one and the same thing. You can't have one without the other. "This *is* the victory that overcometh . . . even our faith." Faith is victory. Victory is faith.

It then follows as logically as light comes with the day, that if we are not living victoriously as Christians, there is something wrong with our faith. We are not exercising it properly. We have not what Paul called "the faith of the Son of God" (Gal. 2:20). Ours may be an intellectual assent to certain doctrines, or a superficial recognition of the saviourhood of the Christ of history. The faith that *is* victory, is different. It is a faith that has come to grips with the Christ of God. It is faith that issues from an immediate contact with Jesus Himself. It is faith that despairs of "self" and is wrecked on God in Christ. It is faith which identifies itself with its Object and finds its all in Him. It is faith which finds in the Lamb of God which taketh away the sin of the world, not only forgiveness, but its very life. It is faith which cries with the apostle of old, "For to me to live is Christ." It is faith which dares to go to Calvary to die so that it is "no longer I . . . but Christ liveth in me." With Christ as our life, we could no more be defeated Christians than we could be beggars and be children of a multi-millionaire.

Once we get a vision of the full implications of Christian faith as those who with Christ have died to sin and with Him have been raised up and made to sit in heavenly places, according to Ephesians 2:3-6, and enter into a life of union with Christ, we can no more be defeated than Christ could be defeated. We are more than conquerors, not in ourselves but through Him who loved us. It is when, with Paul, we are willing to recognize that in us (that is in our flesh) there dwelleth no good thing, and we crucify the flesh (" . . . they that are Christ's have crucified the flesh," Gal. 5:24) that we, too, can say, "Thanks be unto God, which always causeth us to triumph in Christ." We no longer stumble and throw up our hands in amazement over the Saviour's insistence on victory as we have it in the letters to the churches of Asia. He is only saying, after all, "To him that *believeth* will I give to eat of the tree of life, which is in the midst of the paradise of God." "To him that *believeth* will I grant to sit with me in my throne." For this is the victory that overcometh the world, even our faith. To truly believe on the Son of God is to be one with Him. He is the vine, we are the branches. The branch has no other life than that of the vine. When we have no life but Christ, we overcome the world and that not by effort. It must be so, for "whatsoever is born of God overcometh the world."

## Chapter IV

## THE ENEMY

There would not be such an emphasis on the need of victory on the part of the Christian if there were not great forces arrayed against the believer. The Saviour's call to the overcoming life in which the riches of Heaven are placed at the disposition of "him that overcometh," has at its heart a deep implication; namely, that the Christian's enemies are legion, that they are forever at his heels and constantly lurking ready to strike, persistent beyond words to describe. It is nothing short of war—"Drawn swords to the very gates of Heaven," as someone has put it.

Paul tells us in Galatians 5 that the Spirit and the flesh are pitted against each other in mortal combat. Never were opposing forces more relentless in their determination to crush each other. Theirs is an undying enmity. They are as irreconcilable as light and darkness. They are forever at each other's throats. The Christian must overcome the flesh, for if the monster overcomes him and is master, the works of the flesh which are enumerated by the apostle in Galatians 5, hideous as a Satanic brood from Hell, are sure to be in evidence. Some of them may be dressed up in religious garments and appear as holy sectarian zeal, but that does not change their essential character. "Flesh" may mean zeal for a holy Christian cause, a zeal whose motives are wrong. Sectionalism, partisanism, sectarianism, however holy their garments may be, can have no other source than flesh. The Saviour prayed that His followers might be one, which means the slaying of the principle of the self-life. Flesh appears in exceedingly legitimate, refined forms. Still, however refined the forms, it is always and only at enmity with the true Christian spirit. You cannot make a lamb out of a tiger. You cannot make spirit out of flesh.

The world with its vain pomp, its greed of gold, its pleasure madness, its lust for power, its determination to domineer, its racial discriminations, its silly pride, its strife and its defiance of God and neglect of the great salvation provided by His only-begotten Son, the Christ—the world to which Paul said he had been crucified inasmuch as it had crucified his Saviour, is forever at variance with the life which is from Christ. There is no mitigating this variance. No amount of dressing up the world with the attainments of learning, art, and culture can tone down in the least this deep-seated, implacable variance. This sin-cursed world crucified its God-given Redeemer and thereby laid bare its wicked heart. The stuff that the world is made of even at its best when it speaks the language of culture, hides behind the beauties of art and feigns friendship with God, is all laid bare in its true nature by the verities of Calvary; for there it was that the flesh, which as Paul says is enmity toward God, came to its consummate expression. "The carnal mind is enmity against God: for it is not subject to the law of God, neither indeed can be." Golgotha is the overwhelming expression of that fact. Hence, as James puts it, "The friendship of the world is [still] enmity with God." The Christian has forever pressing upon his spirit as an enemy host which besieges a city, the spirit of this world which has declared its hatred of God in the crime of the ages, the crucifixion of His only-begotten Son, in terms so bold and so heinous that no amount of argument to the contrary can ever tone down this fact. The Christian either takes the position of the one who sees himself crucified to the world, or finds himself in the position, at least to a degree, of the one who sold his Master for thirty pieces of silver.

The subtlest of all foes with which the Christian has to deal, is, of course, his own self-love. It was intended that man should love God who made him in His own image for that end. But he turned in on himself. He became infatuated with himself. He sank down into himself. A viler cesspool could not be found. He drew all things to himself, becoming himself the center of the universe, the alpha and the omega of all things. Even after the Christian has received Christ as his Saviour and has been born again, this turning in on self, though mitigated, still has not ceased. Self, like a hundred-headed monster, lifts its ugly head and seeds its own glory, determined to have its own way, come what may. God's plan and God's glory are trampled under foot by the monster as he usurps, rough-shod, his throne. Someone has said that self is like an onion which, however much you peel, still has more that needs to be peeled. In the Christian's struggle he is forever being brought face to face with this inner foe who, because it is his own darling self, is only too often spared.

The Saviour does not bid us deny ourselves *something*. He bids us deny *ourselves*. As suggested in Chapter 2, it is not the bad self which is hardest to deny but rather the *good* self. Paul realized that, after all, there is no such thing as a good self. "I know," he wrote in Romans 7:18, "that in me (that is, in my flesh) dwelleth no good thing." The Christian's greatest battle is won once he recognizes, as did Paul, that in him (that is, in his flesh) dwelleth no good thing.

Then, of course, there is, so to speak, the third person in the trinity of evil; namely, the Devil himself. The believer who is not willing to face squarely the fact of the evil one will never enter upon a full-orbed life of victory, for the reason that those who will not recognize the enemy, taking inventory of his powers and his wiles, can never hope to defeat him. He is a wily foe, quick to seize any advantage that might favor his cause. The greatest of all advantages would be found in going unrecognized.

Here is where many schools of thought regarding victorious Christian living fall short. They are not willing to call for an all-out offensive against the Prince of Darkness. One must be terribly naive, they think, to take seriously the Bible teaching regarding "the powers of darkness" and all that is said of the Christian's conflict with "the rulers of the darkness of this world." But any prudery here is fatal. There is nothing to do but to die to our nice little concepts as to the universe and take God's Word for it, hideous and revolting as it seems. The diagnosis may not be pretty nor attractive, but it will be correct; it will be exact.

The Saviour must be our example here. He faced the foe without first dressing him up with pretty theological terminology making him appear what he is not. He is the Devil with unnumbered hosts of evil spirits at his command who has been in charge of affairs down here in this old world of ours for many a day. "The whole world lieth in the evil one," as I John 5:19 puts it, according to a more exact rendering of the Greek.

The Jews were most religious, but the

Saviour did not mince matters. He told them that they were of their father, the Devil. It is altogether possible to be exceedingly religious and yet under the control of the unseen prince of the world. Where there is pride and lust for vain glory, unholy ambition for office even though it be religious; where there are doctrines contrary to the truth as it is in the Son of God; in a word, where there is uncrucified flesh according to Paul's use of the term in Galatians 5, the evil one is sure to be more or less in the saddle. The Saviour had it out with him on the Cross bruising the head of "that old serpent the Devil." It was here that his rights were annulled and mankind was potentially liberated. It was here that our blessed Redeemer "spoiled principalities and powers, [and] made a shew of them openly triumphing over them in the Cross," as we read in Colossians 2:15. The Christian, who in the evil day when the enemy attacks, does not know how to stand in the strength of the Calvary victory and appropriate its full meaning and apply its glorious power, will surely find the enemy too much for him. He will go down in ignominious defeat overwhelmed by fears and doubts and discouragement. But more of this later. For the present, let it suffice simply to point out the true source of the evil which the Christian must overcome.

Chapter V

# THE SECRET

We have come now to the secret of the victorious life. The "how" of a thing is always the very heart of the matter. It is here that we shall have to divest ourselves of mistaken notions. We shall have to get down to bedrock as to what victory for the Christian is, and as to how it is obtained.

In a sense the word has unfortunate connotations. It conjures up fields of battle. It smells of "the ring." It suggests muscle and courage and struggle. The Christian, we say, must fight and overcome. Yes and no. No, the Christian does not struggle to overcome in his own strength. He does not overcome with the aid of Christ. It is not he plus the aid of his Saviour. He does not come first. It is Christ first and last, with the Christian literally lost in the Saviour. Let us put it this way.

We must never forget that it is not the Christian struggling toward a possible but hard won victory. No. It is the Christian standing in a victory already consummated. A victory consummated for all time, one which when achieved, overcame all—the world, the flesh and the Devil. "Be of good cheer; I have overcome the world," cries the Son of God. "Behold the Lamb of God, which taketh away the sin of the world." In the agonies of the Son of Man as on Calvary's Cross He dies the death of an accursed felon, a new world is born. A new creation is forged. When the Saviour died, as we read in Romans 6, it was the "old man" who too was crucified. It was Satan's hierarchy that was overthrown (see Colossians 2:15, where we read that the powers of darkness were made a shew of openly and utterly defeated). It was the world with all its pomp and lust and pride and bigotry that was exploded as when a balloon is blown up. "Up from the grave He arose with a mighty triumph o'er His foes." And as He ascends, the "new man," as we read in Ephesians 2, ascends with Him to sit with Him in heavenly places and thus to reign.

All talk about victory without first a thorough recognition of God's basis for the Christian's victory, is a hoax. Victory which does not spring from the Calvary victory must eventually fail as when a poor tire is punctured. "Thanks be to God, which giveth us the victory through our Lord Jesus Christ." Victory is as much a gift as is forgiveness. God laid on Him not only our sins but also our sinful nature that it might be undone.

The old man dies and the new creation comes to light (see Gal 2:20). God not only put away guilt in the redemption of His holy Son, but the authority of Satan, the source of man's sin and guilt, was forever annulled (Heb. 2:14). It was not only reconciliation which by the blood of the Cross was wrought—for God was in Christ reconciling the world unto Himself—it was the whole system of evil which Scripture sums up in global fashion when it speaks of "this present evil world" that was overthrown. Paul speaks of the world as a crucified thing—"The world is crucified unto me, and I unto the world."

If literature on this great theme of victorious Christian living fails in giving first this great focus on the infinitely glorious achievement of the Lord Jesus Christ, it is superficial. The Christian's victory does not have as a basis, struggle, because it is already a consummated thing to be accepted by faith in the redemptive achievement of the God-Man, whose "death-resurrection-mid-process," to use Maybe's term, is the experience, judicially before God, of all those who no longer stem from the first Adam but from the second, who is the head of a redeemed race. It is when this judicial position of the Christian is assented to by a hearty amen of faith, that the Holy Spirit has the instrument and material that is needed to place the Christian experimentally in a position of absolute victory in a participation of the death and resurrection of the Son of God.

No, the Christian does not struggle toward a possible victory. He is more than conqueror because his life flows from the triumphant death and resurrection of the Lord Jesus Christ. "And hath raised us up together, and made us sit together in heavenly places" (see Eph. 2:6). Here you have the secret of the victorious Christian life. "This is the victory that overcometh the world, even our faith." That is, having received Christ as Saviour, you already have victory, potentially. You need only discover all the wealth of spiritual riches (unsearchable riches) that are yours in Christ. All things are yours for you are Christ's. He has been made unto you not only justification but also sanctification. "As ye have therefore received Christ Jesus the Lord, so walk ye in him: Rooted and built up in him, and stablished in the faith, as ye have been taught, abounding therein with thanksgiving" (Col. 2:6,7).

## Chapter VI
## THE SECRET (Continued)

To be more than conqueror in such a world as this—one in which temptations of every hue and category assail the believer every moment—is something so amazing, so seemingly impossible, that one is not surprised that even among Christians strong doubts and prejudices exist regarding this matter. And yet, as we saw in the first chapter, God's standard for the believer is none other that one of perennial victory. "Thanks be unto God, which always causeth us to triumph in Christ." There it is. Whittle it down if you like, to fit your mixed, up-and-down, now defeated, now victorious experience. But remember, your experience may be abnormal. It is no rule whereby to measure things. God has laid down a universal rule. His standard is victory, no matter what.

What provokes the doubt is not so much the giants of temptation which are on the outside—that is to say, the world and all its alluring incitements to sin. No. It is the fact that one has multitudinous and multifarious enemies to deal with on the inside. It is one's own flesh. It is one's own self. It is one's own pride. Oh, were it not for that self-pity that is on the inside! Were it not for that self-love, and self-centeredness, which, like blue glasses, gives a false color to everything, or like binoculars ever before one making little insignificant slights, for example, seem great. Were it not for that hyper love of self which keeps one ever seeking for the praise of men and which gives birth to envy, jealousy, fear, resentment and who knows how many other corrupt things that make for defeat. Here's the rub. Is it possible for one to be free from the inner monster which is one's self and which, with subtlest enticements, enslaves and overcomes one's very best efforts to move on a high level of victory?

The answer is an unreserved and unqualified "Yes!" Now let us look squarely at the reason. It is found in the fact that our Lord Jesus Christ, when He wrought redemption on Calvary's Cross, not only bore our sins in His own body on the tree, as Peter puts it in his first epistle, but He also bore us with Himself that in His death we might die. He realized that nothing short of this would meet the exigencies of the case. There had to be a great undoing of our natures, as when you tear down a house to build another in its place. The Saviour took us to the grave and then brought us forth in the power of His resurrection as new creations. Self cannot overcome self. It must die. Nothing short of this will take care of our pride, our self-infatuation, our envy, our restlessness, our resentments and our fussiness. Victory means freedom from the ugly ulcers of self-pity and fear and worry and the love of self. Paul calls it "the flesh."

Romans 6 is the great Bible classic at this juncture. It is the Christian's Magna Carta. Here he reads that he (the old man) was crucified together with Christ; carried to the grave that the old life, leprous because of self, might never again appear. He is commanded to reckon himself dead indeed unto sin and alive unto God, as if his position were exactly that of Jesus, his Lord, which, in the economy of God, it really is. As we read in Ephesians 2: With Christ he has been raised up and with Him he has been made to sit in heavenly places. Christ's ascendancy over the powers of evil is his. All things are under his feet because under Christ's. He reigns because Christ reigns. It was not for himself that the Son of Man went through the Cross to the grave and then to the throne in a glorious resurrection. It was for man. It was as man. It was man. "Ye are dead," writes Paul to the Colossians, "and your life is hid with Christ in God." What happened to Christ, happened to man potentially; to the believer actually, when he enters in by faith.

Here is where we must clarify matters.

When we accept this position of cocrucifixion simply because God says it is ours, whether we feel it or not, then it is that the Holy Spirit has the needed instrument to make victory the supreme fact of our lives. He does not work independently of Christ; He works through the Cross. As A. B. Simpson used to say, "He is the divine undertaker to take us to our graves." He will make Romans 6 and Ephesians 2 and Galatians 2:20—that is, the fact of our identification with Christ in death and resurrection—an unshakable reality in our experience, and we will come into a glorious liberation, a triumphant ascendancy in which victory is ours, not through struggle, but through the participation of Christ. In such an ascendancy, seated with Christ in heavenly places, little things that formerly defeated us are like the waves that beat against Gibralter and have no more effect than these.

This does not mean that there will never again be tempestuous surgings of the life of self. The so-called "wheel of nature" might be set in motion at any moment by some subtle assault of the enemy. Our frail bark is out on a stormy sea. There are sudden and fierce squalls. It is always possible to get out of focus in this position of utter ascendancy. The reason, of course, is not in our perfect Saviour who is "able to keep you from falling, and to present you faultless before the presence of his glory with exceeding joy," but in us; for, like Peter, we get frightened because of the waves and take our eyes off Jesus, whereupon we begin to sink.

We can always come back to our center, nonetheless. We can reaffirm our position. We remember that we have an advocate with the Father, Jesus Christ the righteous. We can always wash our garments and make them white in the precious blood of the Lamb. We expect a fresh application by the Holy Spirit of what has been called "the radium of the Cross," to the freshly discovered cancer of the self-life. It is the function of the Holy Spirit to expose sin; "He will convict the world of sin." A great peace settles down upon our being. We are free once more. The position of ascendancy has been recaptured. We are again more than conquerors through Him that loved us.

This is the meaning of Romans 7 with its cry of despair. It seems strangely out of place in the three great chapters that are the basis of sanctification, but, in point of fact, it is not. Yes, you died according to Romans 6, but you will have to keep on dying lest it be mere doctrine. The flesh must be consigned to the Cross over and over, and as it is, you shout triumphantly as in Romans 8, "The law of the Spirit of life in Christ Jesus hath made me free from the law of sin and death."

## Chapter VII

## OVERCOMING THE POWERS
## OF DARKNESS

There is a trinity of evil—the world, the flesh and the Devil. But the greatest of these is the Devil. With him evil began. He is the prime instigator of the whole process. It was first and foremost for his overthrow that the Saviour came. The first promise in all the sacred Scriptures as to the coming of a redeemer to save mankind focuses upon the struggle with a supernatural being called "that old serpent." The seed of a woman (Christ, as Paul tells us in Galatians 4:4) was to bruise the serpent's head. John tells us that He was manifested to destroy the works of the Devil. In Hebrews 2:14 we read that through death Jesus our Lord destroyed him that has the power of death, that is, the Devil. On the way to the Cross mankind's great Liberator said, "Now is the judgment of this world: now shall the prince of this world be cast out." The Holy Spirit, Jesus said, was to convince the world of this very fact: namely, that the prince of this world has been judged (John 16:11).

It was on the Cross that the blessed Redeemer spoiled principalities and powers and made a shew of them openly triumphing over them in the Cross as we read in Colossians 2:14, 15. Here the rights of the Prince of Darkness, rights conceded by man's sin, rights which resulted in man's oppression and enslavement, were all annulled. The world's Saviour must effectively deal with the underlying cause of man's degradation and bondage. Man's sin and guilt must be wiped out else there could be no effective silencing of the "accuser of the brethren." So long as the evil one had just grounds on which to accuse and oppress man, God Himself could not silence him, for it could not be done by a divine fiat but only by an effective putting away of all sin and guilt in a manner consonant with the holy government of an infinitely adorable and righteous God. Hence the Cross. "Now once in the end of the world hath he [Christ] appeared to put away sin by the sacrifice of himself" (Heb. 9:26).

Now the Christian who hungers after righteousness, and who would be more than conqueror in this wicked world, whose head is the Prince of Darkness, must understand this. He must realize first of all that if he has any doubt as to the efficacy of the Redeemer's sacrifice on Calvary's Cross, it would be better for him not to throw down the gauntlet to man's ancient foe. Victory is not for him.

He does not have the weapons that are needed. If he does not move from Christ's great victory already consummated, he will be an easy prey for the wicked one. Perhaps not along the more flagrant lines of carnal lusts, but the enemy has a more subtle strategy reserved for Christians. With them he works along the line of the good. Now it is good to be sorry for your sins, but the Devil can use this virtue if your sorrow is not mitigated by faith in the efficacy of the Saviour's cleansing blood. If it is allowed to go too far and is not speedily converted into "joy unspeakable and full of glory," by a hearty appropriation of the forgiveness which Scripture assures us is ours because of the Saviour's sacrifice of Himself in our behalf (see Eph. 1:7), then the enemy, who loves nothing more than to lash the believer and drive him to despair by forever reminding him of his sins and by pouring in on him a never-ending stream of accusation, will overcome him.

Here is where the victorious believer learns to be exceedingly wary, refusing absolutely what does not come via Calvary. His "No!" to that sort of thing is most emphatic because he glories only in the Cross. He silences the Devil and cuts himself off from his streams of accusation, on the ground of the Redeemer's precious blood that cleanseth from all sin. Without this his frail bark would be at the mercy of an angry sea and soon sink under its turbulent waters.

Revelation 12 throws a flood of light on this, for here we read that Michael and his angels overcame the dragon and his angels "by the blood of the Lamb, and by the word of their testimony; and they loved not their lives unto the death." You will never know a full-orbed, perennial victory until you stand right there, for there is nothing that so debilitates the believer as a sense of guilt and condemnation. The Devil knows this and pours it on. But as Christians we can say: It is a lie. For there is therefore now no condemnation to them that are in Christ. And if the Saviour bore in His body on the tree our sins, they are no longer on us. They are gone forever. It is not God, who has promised to remember them no more, who throws them up to us, but the Devil. We must recognize this fact and stand foursquare on Calvary's consummated verities. And as we do, Satan flees.

This is not all. Note that those who overcame the dragon and his angels "loved not their lives unto the death." That is to say, there was no self-love. All self-love gives Satan ground on which to work. Uncrucified flesh is gunpowder into which he will sooner or later throw a match, and a terrible conflagration may result. The victorious Christian must stand where the Saviour stood when He said, "The Prince of this world cometh, and hath nothing in me" (John 14:30). Oh how the enemy fought in an effort to provoke something in Jesus that would give him ground. Back of the mocking, the spitting, the cruel scourging, the reviling, the blasphemous jeering and all was the Prince of Darkness of this world whose works the Saviour had come to destroy. But it was all in vain. The wicked one found nothing in Jesus.

Now we must be able to say: the evil one hath nothing in me. If he can find something in you that he can exploit—some ill-will, some envy, some unwillingness to forgive a brother that may have wronged you, some secret pride, some unholy prejudice, some unclean lust after the praise of men; in a word, what Paul calls "flesh" (see Gal. 5: 19-21)—you will most surely go under in the hour of conflict. But you say: How can I stand where Jesus stood? I answer: By a recognition and a full appropriation of what He wrought for you on Calvary. He took you with Himself to the Cross that the old man might be destroyed. You were raised up and made to sit with Him in heavenly places (see Rom. 6 and Eph. 2). Over the new-creation life Satan has no power. It is the old man who is his workshop. Are you living on the ground of the uncrucified old creation? If so, then you are as vulnerable to Satan's fiery darts as a cotton rag to machine gun bullets.

A student in our seminary came one day

to talk with the president saying that he could no longer continue his studies. Life was unbearable in the seminary as the students were forever razzing him. They gave him no peace. The president asked the young man to hang his hat, which he had in his hand, on the wall. Now there was no peg or nail to hang it on. The young man remonstrated that he could find nothing to hang his hat on. He was told to hang it anyway. It fell to the ground. The president ordered the young man again to hang his hat on the wall. When again it fell to the ground, the young man said, "Sir, what do you mean by this?" The answer was, "If the students did not find in you so many susceptibilities, so much regard for self, so much secret vanity, they would leave you in peace." The student saw the point and left the room a changed man. The students molested him no longer. If Satan can find anything in us to hang on to, he will surely knock us out in the testing time. We are invulnerable only as, identified with Christ in His death, we cry, "It is no longer I, but Christ liveth in me."

## Chapter VIII

## THE AUTHORITY
## OF THE BELIEVER

There is no possibility of living a full-orbed victorious life if the Christian fails to enter into the meaning of such passages as Luke 10:17-19 where the Saviour says: "Behold I give unto you power (Greek—authority) to tread on serpents and scorpions, and over all the power of the enemy: and nothing shall by any means hurt you" (vs.19). The sinner who knows not Christ as Saviour may have authority because of office among men, but in the spiritual order his work is nil. He is a slave because of sin. Sin has placed him under Satan's sceptre. He could no more command demons than he could command the stars. They would turn on him as of old the demons turned on the sons of Sceva, who sought to cast them out, and tore off their clothes and overcame them.

With the Christian it is otherwise however. To him the Saviour says: If ye say to this mountain, be thou removed and doubt not in your heart; what ye say shall be done (Mark 11:23). Of course, He is not speaking of material mountains. Mountains in the Scriptures represent kingdoms, authority, rule, empires. It is the kingdom and authority of the Prince of the darkness of this world to which the Saviour refers. When the seventy went forth to preach and in Jesus' Name to heal and to cast out demons upon their return, He said, "I beheld Satan as lightning fall from heaven."

Now the spiritual principles involved are as simple as the most ordinary mathematical proposition. Two and two are four could not be more basic or more simple. The underlying principles are these: Christ Jesus the Lord was manifested to destroy the works of the Devil (I John 3:8); He bruised the serpent's head on Calvary's Cross, fulfilling the very first promise in Holy Writ regarding the coming of a Saviour; and there He spoiled principalities and powers and made a shew of them openly triumphing over them in the Cross, as we read in Colossians 2:14, 15. This was the primary purpose of His coming—the rest would logically and inevitably flow from this crowning achievement.

The believer steps into the glorious fruits of this crowning achievement the moment he receives Christ as his personal Saviour. "But as many as received him, to them gave he power [authority] to become the sons of God, even to them that believe on His Name" (John 1:12). All authority, said the

Saviour after His resurrection, had been given unto Him, both in Heaven and upon earth. That, of course, is true. But you cannot be associated with Him in the manner in which Scriptures say the true believer is associated (see Rom. 6:11, John 15, also Eph. 2:4-6, Col. 3:33, Gal 2:20), without a participation in the Saviour's authority. We have been made priests and kings unto God. We have been raised up with Christ and made to sit together with Him in heavenly places. We reign in life by One, even Jesus Christ (see Rom. 5:17). Where the Head is, there also is the body. All things were put under the Head's feet; therefore under the body's feet. The Head is "above all principality, and power, and might, and dominion, and every name that is named, not only in this world, but also in that which is to come"; then the body also is above. This is the plain teaching of Ephesians 1:15-23.

"Behold I give unto you power . . . over all the power of the enemy" (Luke 10:19). Once the believer gets that fixed in his mind and heart and begins to act on it, then, indeed, he becomes more than conqueror. He no longer quails before the Enemy. Like David before the giant Philistine who had defied Israel's hosts and, blaspheming her Lord, had made her army tremble, he says: "I come to thee in the name of the Lord of hosts, the God of the armies of Israel, whom thou hast defied . . . This day will the Lord deliver thee into mine hand; and I will smite thee."

Once a little cat that was being madly chased by a big dog, suddenly stopped and, turning on the dog, bristled defiance and arched as if to strike. The result was that the dog fell back, cowed and slunk away defeated. The believer, who would be victorious in all the circumstances of life, must no longer cower before Satan. He must realize that the enemy is a defeated foe. He must once and for all settle it that according to God's Holy Word, the Devil's rights have all been annulled. Taking his stand firmly on such a text as, for example, Hebrews 2:14, where we read that through death the Redeemer destroyed him that had the power of death, that is the Devil, he exercises authority in the Name of his all-triumphant Lord. If, in the hour of conflict with the powers of darkness, he does this, he will find that he is able to move mountains—mountains of Satanic oppression. He finds that as he withstands in the evil day according to Ephesians 6:13, and having done all stands, he comes off the field of battle more than conqueror.

There is no need talking about victorious Christian living unless we are willing to face the fact that as Christians we are out of our element here in this world. We are living in enemy territory. The prince of this world with whom are the demon forces of the powers of darkness, will "make it hot for us," for though judged and defeated at Calvary, he still holds sway. He holds sway because many millions are yet in unbelief. The victory is patent only as we enter in by faith. Even Christians may be in bondage because of deception or ignorance of the full scope of their inheritance in Christ, or because they have not, according to Romans 6:11, reckoned themselves dead to sin and alive unto God through Jesus Christ the Lord. Where there is sin, Satan finds ground upon which to stand. Where there is uncrucified flesh, Satan has material to work on.

We are in enemy territory, I repeat, but we can be more than conquerors by taking our place with Christ in death and resurrection. We must learn to stand on resurrection ground, reckoning dead the old-creation life over which Satan has power, and living in the new creation over which Satan has no power whatever. This is the fundamental law of victorious Christian living. From this position of oneness with Christ ("Christ within, the hope of glory," Col. 1:27), we exercise delegated authority. We make patent the Redeemer's Calvary victory—surrounded as we are by demon forces that strike when we least expect it—by an act of faith. As we stand unshaken, the enemy flees, for the Holy Spirit bears witness to the fact that he has been judged and overthrown as we see in John 16:11.

General Wainwright tells of his great suffering in the Manchurian concentration camp after the fall of Bataan. Japanese prison keepers made him an object of their mockery day by day. He knew nothing of what was happening in the outside world. He became a skeleton, as it were—a broken, crushed, hopeless, starving man. One day an airplane landed in the camp, and a colonel of the allied forces marched up to General Wainwright telling him that Japan had been defeated. Imagine the effect of such news upon the spirit of this dying man. The colonel, having delivered his message, took to the skies once more. When Japanese prison keepers, not knowing what had happened, returned to mock and buffet the general as formerly, he said, "No, I am in command here. These are my orders." The prison keepers, shocked beyond words, understood that the general had been informed of the Allied Victory. From that moment General Wainwright was king.

Have you been informed of the victory of your Saviour in the greatest conflict of the ages? Have you heard His voice, "Behold I give unto you power . . . over all the power of the enemy"? Then rise up to assert your rights. You are now a king. Rise up to reign. Give the command of faith. Never again go under when the enemy comes to oppress. Claim the victory in Jesus' Name. Say: I am in command here. Give your orders. The enemy will flee, and you will live victoriously no matter how many, or in what manner, the demons come out against you. Furthermore, you will learn to liberate others. And that as a Christian is your mission.

## Chapter IX

## VICTORY—THE EQUIVALENT
## OF OBEDIENCE

We cannot underscore too strongly the fact that it is by grace that we are saved. Salvation is indeed the gift of God. It can truly be said that it was all wrought out on Calvary by the Son of God when He shed His precious blood for the remission of sins and for the redemption of mankind.

It is one thing to be saved, however, and another to maintain an experience of actual victory over the world, the flesh and the Devil. It is one thing to be justified according to Romans 5 and another to be "made free from sin . . . [and] have your fruit unto holiness," according to Romans 6:22. To be more than conquerors through Him that loved us according to Romans 8:37, we must enter into a life of fullness in Christ through the gateway of an utter identification with Him in death and in resurrection. The price we pay is obedience. In a sense it costs us nothing; in another it costs us everything.

"We have received grace . . . for obedience to the faith," writes Paul in Chapter 1 of Romans, the fifth verse. We read in Hebrews 5:9 that our Lord became the author of eternal salvation unto all them that obey Him. Grace is not divorced from works, for it issues in a life of obedience. Every thought is to be brought into captivity to the obedience of Christ (II Cor. 10:5).

The basic law of victorious Christian living is expressed for all time in Paul's classic: "Not I, but Christ" of Galatians 2:20. To the degree in which it is not I, but Christ, will the Christian be swept along by the heavenly stream of victory. Paul could say, "I can do all things through Christ which strengtheneth me," but the basic rule of his life was "Lord, what wilt thou have me to do?"

Here you have the reason for so much defeat in the ranks of Christians. The "more than conqueror" affirmation of Romans 8 leaves them cold. They are swept along by the tide of worldliness, helpless before the monster the Bible denominates "the flesh," only too often dancing to the Devil's tune, knowing little or nothing of the meaning of such a categorical as: "Thanks be unto God, which always causeth us to triumph in Christ"; because they have never crowned Christ Lord of all in a life of irrevocable obedience to Him. Victory means a day-by-day and a moment-by-moment life of full surrender and obedience to Christ, a willingness to be nothing, that He may be All.

F. B. Meyer tells how he entered into a life of victory after years of controversy with his Lord and Master over what he calls "the last key." The Saviour, he says, would stand at the door of his heart pleading for the surrender of the last key. "But, Lord," the preacher would argue, "I have given you all the keys." To which the Saviour would reply, "All but one." And so the controversy went on for years, until, as Meyer says, one day he realized that his Lord had asked for the last time the key which he had been so unwilling to yield. It was then, Meyer says, he came to his senses so to speak, shocked beyond measure by the fact that his resistance had so grieved his patient, loving Redeemer. It broke his proud heart, and he cried, "Do not go away; I am now willing. Here, I give thee the last key." From then on it would be absolute obedience in all things to his Lord. In that hour, Meyer says, he entered a life of victory.

If as a Christian you would enter into a life of perennial victory, this issue will have to be raised. The Saviour will not, dare not, must not, cannot spare you. It will not be raised in the same way, of course, but the issue will be forced upon you, and you will have to surrender the last key. You will have to sell out utterly. Jesus now reigns supreme; time, money, thoughts, imagination, tongue, loved ones, all is brought under His glorious sway. The Lord commands (I should say, Infinite Love whispers); you obey.

You no longer think of victory, nor do you seek it. You seek no experience. You seek only Christ. You have lost sight of self. Like the apostles on the Mount of Transfiguration, you see no one save Jesus only. The inevitable consequence is that the "river of water of life, clear as crystal, [that] proceedeth out of the throne of God and of the Lamb" invades your being and sweeps you along on a glorious stream of victory. Depression is now a thing of the past. Fear is gone. "Perfect love casteth out fear." Envy dare not raise its ugly head, and if it does, it is immediately taken to the Cross. Death would only mean the full realization of heaven's eternal richness and beauty in the reception of the crown of life. You find that His commands, as Spurgeon used to say, are His enablings; for rivers of living water flow from your innermost being. On a woman's tombstone were found the words: "She did what she could." So you do what you could not, for Christ is now your life and nothing is too hard for the Lord.

## Chapter X

## FROM VICTORY CONSUMMATED—
## NOT TO A POSSIBLE VICTORY

It cannot be overemphasized that the Christian does not struggle toward a possible victory. No! He proceeds from a victory already achieved. He follows in the train of the Lord Jesus Christ celebrating a victory long since consummated, as Conybeare's rendering of II Corinthians 2:14 puts it. That is why John in his First Epistle General so stoutly affirms that faith is the victory that overcometh the world.

We think of victory in terms of the world. The word, I repeat, really has a bad connotation. It savours of the battlefield and of the pride of man. The non-Christian, too, wants victory. There is nothing more alluring, nothing more satisfactory, nothing more desirable. But the Christian's victory is different. It has nothing whatever to do with carnal weapons; it does not lift its proud head over the ruins of a fellow-man's defeat; it humiliates no one. The Christian's victory is not over others, but over himself. His sword is drawn, not to slay his fellow-man, but to slay himself. He wins by losing. He triumphs by being defeated. He lives by dying. His crown is a crown of thorns. His throne is a Cross. His weapon is not strength but weakness. His victory is not found in establishing his own cause but in establishing that of his fellow-men: the poor, the sick, the disinherited, the brokenhearted, the wayward, the lost. This may be foolishness to men. But we must not forget that "the foolishness of God is wiser than men; and the weakness of God is stronger than men" (I Cor. 1:25).

Let us come back to our initial statement: "Thanks be unto God, which always causeth us to triumph in Christ . . . " The Christian can triumph *always* for the reason that he proceeds on the basis of a victory already consummated. He can look forward to a life of victory, come what may, in wealth or in poverty, in health or in sickness, in life or in death, because his victory is not his own. It comes from Another. It was consummated by the Son of God, who had constituted Himself the Son of Man under conditions so adverse, in the face of such a flood-tide of demon forces from Hell itself, with all that there is of evil in this wicked old world of ours vomiting forth its hate and filth and death to overthrow, were it possible, this One, who as man, had come to espouse the seemingly hopeless cause of man. "Up from the grave He arose with a mighty triumph o'er His foes."

His: "Be of good cheer; I have overcome the world," stands as it has stood for twenty centuries and will stand forever. Christ's victory took into account every foe that could ever threaten the eternal welfare of man: death, hell, sin, guilt, fear, Satan, sorrow, etc., etc., were all defeated. "Fear not," cries our resurrected Lord, "I am he that liveth, and was dead; and, behold, I am alive for evermore, Amen; and have the keys of hell and of death" (Rev. 1:17,18).

Now here is the crux of the matter. Let us be very plain. ("Seeing then that we have such hope, we use great plainness of speech" II Cor. 3:12.) Christ's victory is man's victory. He wrought it all out as man. He achieved it all as Representative Man. He is the second Adam. As in the first we died; in the second we live. He "was manifested to destroy the works of the Devil." They have been destroyed, and it was Man who destroyed them. As Son of Man, Christ the Lord is bone of your bone, flesh of your flesh. When He arose, you arose. His ascendancy over "all principality, and power, and might, and dominion, and every name that is named, not only in this world, but also in that which is to come," is your ascendancy. The Christian has been quickened together with Christ and with Him has been raised up that together with Him he might sit in heavenly places (see Eph. 2:1, 5, 6). All this, that in the ages to come

65

He might shew the exceeding riches of His grace in His kindness toward us through Christ Jesus (Eph. 2:7).

That is why the Christian who enters into all that God has for him in Christ, does not struggle toward a possible victory. He begins where the Representative Man, the Lord Jesus Christ, left off. The battle has already been won. The Christian's victory is nothing more nor less than an Amen of faith to the great all-comprehensive victory which Christ consummated at Calvary in his name, in his behalf, for his sake when He came to champion his (humanly speaking) desperate, hopeless, forlorn cause.

So, Christian, I counsel thee to give up the fight if in your own strength you have been struggling to obtain a victory which you seem never quite able to achieve in spite of prayers and tears and effort and consecration and what not. You do not have to climb this stony, thorn-infested, unscalable mountain. You can begin at the top. Strange as that may seem, it is true. You can begin where Jesus left off. You need only say Amen (may the Holy Spirit enable you) to that which God declares as fact, that it was your humanity which Christ, who for you died, and in whom you died, took to the Cross and via the empty tomb to the throne. "Ye are dead and your life is hid with Christ in God" (Col. 3:3).

"Ye are come to mount Sion, and unto the city of the living God, the heavenly Jerusalem, and to an innumerable company of angels, to the general assembly and church of the firstborn, which are written in Heaven, and to God the Judge of all, and to the spirits of just men made perfect, and to Jesus, the mediator of the new covenant . . . " (Heb. 12:22-24). It does not say: if you struggle and pray hard enough you will come at last. No. It says that you have already arrived. You have arrived because Jesus has arrived. You have arrived in Him. His victory is your victory.

Here prayer of the ordinary type, which is somewhat of a beggar's attitude, breaks down. Prayer has its place, but here it is out of place unless it be praise. We must learn the lesson of affirmation. We can't go wrong by affirming what God affirms. We need not ask God to seat us in heavenly places far above all, in a victorious position. We are already there if we are, as true believers, in Christ. We need only affirm it. This is faith. This was Paul's method. "I can do all things through Christ which strengtheneth me." "I am crucified [together] with Christ: nevertheless I live; yet not I, but Christ liveth in me: and the life which I now live in the flesh I live by the faith of the Son of God, who loved me, and gave himself for me." "The law of the Spirit of life in Christ Jesus hath made me free from the law of sin and death." "We are more than conquerors through him that loved us." It looks like presumption. But there is no presumption in faith. Pride is the handmaid of unbelief. We get nowhere by begging for something the Lord says we already have.

How clearly this comes to light in Paul's prison experience at Philippi. He and his companions have come to Macedonia in obedience to a divine call. But they are met with terrific opposition. They are beaten and thrown into prison. They are thrown into the "inner prison" and their feet made fast in the stocks. It is midnight. What an unhappy lot is now theirs. Is this the man who claimed to be more than conqueror and who said that believers were always to triumph? Why this is defeat of the deepest dye.

Wait a minute. This is not defeat. This is victory. Paul knows that God's disappointments are really His appointments and that all things work together for good to them that love Him. We read that Paul and Silas prayed, but it was prayer that is praise, for they "sang praises unto God." We all know the outcome. The foundations of the prison were shaken by an earthquake. The prison keeper himself, casting himself at the apostle's feet, cried out, saying, "Sirs, what must I do to be saved?" That very night the prison keeper is baptized and rejoices, believing in God with all his house. But it was victory all the way. First invisible and then visible. First it was in spirit and then in fact. Paul and Silas had never come down in the midst of the scourging, and the darkness and the prison stench, from a position of ascendancy in Christ. They were still more than conquerors while being beaten. They were still more than conquerors while being beaten. They do not ask for victory. They praise God for the victory that is theirs in Christ. The earthquake, and all the rest which the Lord saw fit to work in vindication of His servants, were only the visible reflections in time and space of a yet greater victory; namely, the victory of the Son of God which had been maintained in spirit.

It was Donald Hankey, who learned to maintain the Christian's victory in the midst of the vicissitudes of war, that said in *The Student at Arms,* "This *is* victory, to know that God alone matters."

## Chapter XI

## IN THE EVIL DAY—VICTORY

It seems strange at first thought that the Ephesian Epistle which presents the ideal Church as the body of Christ, "the fullness of him that filleth all in all"; the Church whose position is in heavenly places where she sits far above all with Him who is the head—it seems passing strange and altogether incongruous, I repeat, that the Ephesian Epistle should close with a call to arms. There is the shrill note of the bugle calling the soldiers of Christ to battle. We are told that we wrestle not with flesh and blood; but that the fiercest conflicts are with supernatural powers—principalities and powers, the rulers of the darkness of this world, spiritual wickedness in high places. We are exhorted to put on the whole armour of God that we may be able to stand against the wiles of the Devil and to withstand in the evil day.

Yet there is nothing far-fetched or incongruous about this. We may not like it, but it rings true. The more advanced the Christian, the fiercer the conflict. It is when we take our place with Christ in His death and are shorn of the flesh-life, and in the participation of His resurrection learn to sit with Him in heavenly places, that we first get a correct view of the real fight. We see the invisible foe. Satan and his hosts loom up before us, and the battle begins in the heavenlies with demon forces.

It was so with Israel after she crossed Jordan and entered into the Promised Land. It was then that war in the fullest sense began. Israel must now meet the giants of the land; the sons of Anak. Jericho must be overthrown; walled cities leveled, and kings brought out of caves in which they had taken refuge, and beheaded. Crossing Jordan into the Promised Land meant war, not peace.

The Christian who through indentification with Christ in death and resurrection enters into the Promised Land of a life of fullness and of victory finds himself up against the forces of Hell pitted against Christ and His Church. He is now a target for the powers of darkness. He is now a menace as never before to the Enemy of Christ, the rulers of the darkness of this world. He comes to realize as never before that here in this world, whose head is the Prince of Darkness, he is living in enemy territory and that he is going to be made to feel it. He is subject to barrages from the pit. He will be attacked by the demons of the underworld. It will no longer be primarily, as before, simply a question of temptation. That question has been settled, though of course he may still be tempted, for, as we read in Galatians 5:24, "They that are Christ's have crucified the flesh with the affections and lusts."

He must now fashion a strategy of a very different order. Carnal weapons are now of no value. They must be weapons mighty through God to the pulling down of strongholds (II Cor. 10:4). He is called upon now "to withstand in the evil day." That is not the language of mere defense warfare. He comes to realize that there is no defense like attack. In the evil day he is to strike at the one who lies behind mere circumstances and in the Name of Jesus rout the foe.

That will take practice and a hardening, as it were, in battle. There will not be wanting opportunities, for the enemy is wily and persistent. It is Luke who remarks that the Devil, after the Saviour's forty days of fasting and conflict in the desert, departed from Him "for a season." He will come back to strike under other circumstances perhaps more favorable, feeling out the vulnerable points in your armour. He may very likely leave you for a considerable time, letting blessings flow in unhindered, just to get you off your guard. Then when you least expect it, and when days of spiritual ease and delight have led you to believe that the days of conflict are over, and your position in Christ can never again be challenged, and, as a consequence, your fighting spirit has waned, the blow falls. The evil day is upon you. It came to Job.

The enemy will bring about a horrible feeling of depression. Darkness falls like night upon your spirit. You feel abandoned of God. You cry out for help, but no answer comes. Now is when the enemy whispers doubts. Fiery darts pierce your armour. The suggestion is made that you have been forsaken because of your sins.

Now you will come to know the enemy as "the accuser of the brethren." A flood of accusations pour in upon you. You cry out for forgiveness, but the flood only increases. It is not a time to confess old sins long since blotted out by the blood of the Lamb and therefore no longer remembered by the Most High. This is the Devil's trick. It is a time for a thorough girding on of the whole armour of God. It is a time to examine your armour to make sure no weapon either of defense or of offense may be missing. It is a time to withstand. It is a time to resist the Devil. It is a time to remember that your Lord on Calvary bruised the Serpent's head, and that his rights have all been annulled. It is a time to rise up and throw off the Satanic lethargy and to claim the victory. Learn at such a time to exercise executive authority. You are a king unto God made such by your Redeemer. You have a right to "say unto this mountain, be thou removed." And if you doubt not in your heart what you say shall be done (see Mark 11:23, also Luke 10:19, and I John 4:4).

This is not a pleasant theme. In fact it is humiliating. Those who are out after "religious swank" will refuse to accept. But I am addressing soldiers whose passion is victory. The great theme we are studying makes imperative a frank facing of facts. Soldiers must know the strategy and strength and nature of the enemy. There can be no victorious Christian living if we will not do as Paul says in the last chapter of Ephesians where we are told to put on the whole armour of God to stand against the wiles of the Devil.

The atmosphere of the world seems charged today as never before with demon forces. Mountains of Satanic depression are weighing down upon the nations. It is becoming increasingly difficult for the Christian to maintain a victorious spirit. It is for just such an hour as this that Jesus the Lord gives His assuring promise: "Because thou hast kept the word of my patience, I also will keep thee from the hour of temptation, which shall come upon all the world, to try them that dwell upon the earth" (Rev. 3:10).

The Saviour's "Be of good cheer; I have overcome the world," still stands. When Paul wrote: "Nay, in all these things we are more than conquerors through him that loved us,"

74

he had in mind adversaries no less terrifying than those we must face today. Hear him please: "For thy sake we are killed all the day long; we are accounted as sheep for the slaughter." He speaks of tribulation, distress, persecution, famine, nakedness, peril and sword. In II Corinthians he speaks of being pressed out of measure, above strength, insomuch that he despaired even of life. He languished for years in Roman prisons. Yet we never hear of him admitting even the bare possibility of defeat. He insists to the very end that it was ever and only victory, thanking God who always caused him to triumph in Christ (II Cor. 2:14).

It did not always look like victory, for the standards of the world are different. From the outside it looked like the most shameful defeat. But on the inside he was more than conqueror. His victory was of the order of Calvary. It may be shame and humiliation and weakness and suffering and death. God does not always see fit to deliver us from these things; but He has made ample provision in Christ who was made unto us "wisdom, and righteousness, and sanctification, and redemption," that in these things we may be patient and longsuffering and forgiving as was our Lord in the days of His flesh. It was from prison that Paul wrote: "Rejoice in the Lord alway: and again I say, Rejoice."

## Chapter XII

## THE ANSWER OF DEATH

This is a Principle enunciated by the Apostle Paul in II Corinthians the first chapter which we must take fully into account, if we would know a full-orbed victory—more than conquerors through Him that loved us. The apostle makes mention of a great trial which came to him in Asia. He does not go into details and therefore leaves us wondering as to what particular trouble he may be referring. It may have been the stoning in Lystra where he was left for dead. However it may have been, he affirms that he and his companions were pressed beyond measure insomuch that they despaired even of life.

Now comes the startling word: "But we had the sentence of death in ourselves, that we should not trust in ourselves, but in God which raiseth the dead: Who delivered us from so great a death, and doth deliver: in whom we trust that he will yet deliver us." Paul's answer was death. The result was a virtual resurrection. He *was* delivered. He said that he *was being* delivered. He expressed the conviction that he *would be* delivered.

Here you have the heart of Paul's theology as regards the Christian life. He conceived of the Christian as one identified with his Saviour. To him the Saviour's death, as Son of Man, Representative Man, was the Christian's death, "Our old man is crucified with him"; the Saviour's burial is the Christian's burial, "We have been planted together in the likeness of his death"; the Saviour's resurrection is the Christian's resurrection, "God . . . hath quickened us together with Christ, and hath raised us up together"; the Saviour's ascension and exaltation at the right hand of the Father is the Christian's ascension and exaltation, "God . . . made us sit together in heavenly places in Christ."

This was no mere theory with Paul. With him doctrine was not simply a matter of the head but must become incarnate. Here was his opportunity to prove in actual experience what had been revealed to him doctrinally. His answer to this great trouble which caused him to despair even of life would be his identification with his Lord in the aforementioned "death - resurrection - mid - process." "What have I to fear," says Paul in effect, "have I not already died to the world? Is it not crucified unto me in my Redeemer's Cross? Have I not been raised up with my Saviour in the power of His resurrection? Is not my life hid with Christ in God? Why, I have already experienced the world's worst, the Devil's uttermost in the participation of my

Redeemer's Cross. I have already been released in spirit from death's dark domain. If the Lord permits this to issue in actual physical dissolution, it will only mean a yet fuller participation in the life of Heaven which is already mine. If the divine purposes are not yet fulfilled in me, and there is further work for me to do, then the power of Christ's resurrection which is mine in spirit, will also be mine in the material order, and I shall be delivered." And so it was. Paul and His companions were delivered. The answer was death. They trusted in God which raiseth the dead.

There you have the principle—the warp and woof of New Testament teaching regarding the Christian life. You cannot live the victorious Christian life without the answer of death. You will find yourself again and again in circumstances offering no hope. There is no way out. Defeat stares you in the face. The Devil has penned you up. Now is the time to sing. You are not trusting in circumstances but in God which raiseth the dead. Choose His will in the matter. Make it a definite transaction with God. If He has further work for you to do; if you have not yet finished your God-ordained course, you will experience something akin to the Cross and the empty tomb. The forces that operate in the Cross and the empty tomb, operate in you if you are a Christian. Let your answer be Paul's answer of death. If you do, you will also have Paul's: "God which raiseth the dead . . . delivered us."

It was one of the great Scottish divines who, when told that he was to be killed (those were days when Christians suffered persecution for their faith), replied, saying, "What, I am to be killed? They cannot hurt me. I have already died." His was the answer of death. Here is the golden key to infinite treasures. Let your answer be death, not only in the great crises when you despair of life, but in a moment-by-moment participation in your Redeemer's Cross. Get it clearly and definitely and eternally fixed in your heart and mind that God in His wondrous love, His holy economy, sweet and blessed beyond words to express, has already taken you clear out of this old world's sin and pain and shame and death. He says categorically (Col. 3:3), "Ye are dead and your life is hid with Christ in God."

If we would as Christians only proceed on this basis living on resurrection ground, because the new creation began with the Saviour's resurrection, keeping steadily for every situation the determined answer of death; we would experience a stream of victory such as we never dreamed possible this side of the portals of Heaven. Let me give a simple, homely illustration applying the principle, not as did Paul to a great trial, but to a little everyday stumbling block.

Let us presume that I have had my feelings hurt. Just remember that more Christians go on the rocks, defeated, over the nasty little thing we call "hurt feelings" than over the so-called great crises which test the very fibre of the soul. I have been slighted. I have not been given the place I feel I merit, or I have been treated inconsiderately, unjustly. Self has been wounded. My opinions and feelings have not been consulted. As a result I have begun to sink. I am being defeated, not by a monster, but by a mere fly. And yet it is no less defeat. A "scum" covers my spirit formerly free and rejoicing. I have sunk down into the so-called "vessel of the soul." I have become soulish. The stream of eternal life from the throne and from the Lamb has ceased to flow in and out of my being. My step has become heavy, and my face now carries an unhappy, darkened look. I am plainly defeated. Wounded pride did it. I looked at my self and took my eyes off Jesus my Lord.

How different all would have been if my answer had been the sublime answer of death! I would immediately have said, "They crucified my Lord—this is nothing. It is my chance to go a little deeper into the fellowship of my Saviour's sufferings, being made conformable unto His death. The result will be a fuller participation of His resurrection.

Thank You, Lord, for these things that have hurt. Bless those who have hurt me. I forgive as Thou didst forgive. I am deeply grateful for this reminder of my nothingness. I am willing to be nothing that Thou mightest be all. Amen!"

Now when our answer is the answer of the Cross, nothing can hurt us. We immediately turn everything into blessing. We go up by going down. We triumph through death. We feed on the holy Cross and live. The kick backward was really a kick forward. The hurt feeling is immediately staunched in the Saviour's death which the Holy Spirit has freshly applied, and the stream of eternal life from the throne flows richer and fuller than ever. Our concern is that Christ be glorified, the rest does not matter.

You would be surprised what this principle would do for Christian work, the Christian ministry, or missions if applied. I have lived for thirty years with missionaries, and how precious they are—God's peers; but their greatest enemy, as it is with all Christians, regardless, is pride. When they do not have the answer of death, a glad participation in Christ's death and resurrection, they know much of defeat even in the midst of great blessing.

It wasn't until Job's answer was the answer of death that God "turned his captivity" and raised him up from the "dunghill" where he sat scraping his reeking, leprous skin. We read that it was when Job prayed for his friends that the Lord turned his captivity. How those friends had comforted, no— irritated him with their veiled accusations. How he had defended himself; how he had sought to justify himself. And he *was* innocent. That is what made it so hard. Job drinks the very dregs from the cup of the gall of bitterness. Job finally gets his eyes off self looking up to his Redeemer. "I know that my Redeemer liveth." Job "dies out to self," to use an old but ever blessed phrase of the divines of former days. Job ceases to think of self; to defend and justify self. Job suddenly swings out into universals, praying for friends who had so deeply wounded his feelings. He gives the answer of death. And God turns his affliction. Victory.

## Chapter XIII

## IN THE HOUR OF DEFEAT

I wish I did not have to write this chapter. But if I failed to write it, I should be a fraud, I should not be a true interpreter of the Word, nor of Christian experience. It would seem perhaps that I am now retracting and taking back, in part at least, what has been said in the foregoing chapters. But such is not the case. Rather do I hope to corroborate, establishing from the negative side, the positive experience of victory.

The possibility of defeat, even of the most victorious Christians, is admitted with utter frankness in Holy Writ. It is evidenced, sad to say, only too often. I John 2:1 will be our Scriptural basis: "And if any man sin, we have an advocate with the Father, Jesus Christ the righteous." Here the apostle admits the possibility of defeat. Note carefully that he does not say, "When you sin . . . " He does not admit the necessity, for abundant provisions have been made in and through Christ to maintain an unbroken chain of victory. "Thanks be unto God, which always causeth us to triumph in Christ . . ."—stands. We have no thought of altering or weakening *that*. But *that* is the divine side of the case. That is what God is able to do. Here we have the unsearchable riches of Christ at the disposal of the believer. The "if" we are raising applies only to the human aspect of appropriation.

"If any man sin . . ." If your boy gets sick, call a doctor. You do not expect sickness for a rolicking, romping, happy, healthy boy; but should he fall ill, you call the doctor. It is not the normal thing. The normal thing is health. The normal thing for the Christian is health—robust, spiritual health; a joyous overflowing life of joy and love in and through Christ the Lord with victory as a natural, spontaneous fruit. But Christians, even the most victorious, often fail to take full possession of their possessions in Christ and as a consequence may suffer defeat before the onslaughts of the world, the flesh, and the Devil.

Victory is not a static thing which once obtained makes it possible for the believer to be less watchful as regards tomorrow's temptations. The Devil will suit his wiles in an ever more subtle approach to our stage of growth, our advanced position of victory in Christ. It is still true that he that thinketh he standeth must take heed lest he fall. We never reach a place in the Christian life where it is no longer necessary to watch and pray lest we fall into temptation.

A constant coming back in spirit to our Center, which is Christ the Lord, is our only safeguard. The monster ever lurks near ready to lift his ugly head. Pride is a very subtle thing. "Our old man *is* crucified with him" (Rom. 6:6). The command, "Mortify therefore your members which are upon the earth . . ." Following on the heels of the categorical "Ye are dead and your life is hid with Christ in God," makes it only too clear that victory is a process, an unfolding flower which may be tragically blighted should we fail to maintain a steady focus upon the Cross of Christ. It will be helpful to those who aspire for uninterrupted victory in Christ to learn to keep short accounts. You must keep checking. John writes to victorious Christians when he says, "Beloved, believe not every spirit, but try the spirits whether they are of God." Let nothing pass without examination.

The Church has not known a more truly victorious Christian than the sainted Frances Havergal, author of so many of our most precious hymns. But Miss Havergal was not always the rejoicing, victorious Christian that she was in later years. On the contrary, she was long a sad, burdened, defeated soul. Melancholia was her great enemy. She was unhappy; her life was lived under the cloud caused by an undue concern in view of her "many faults." Her blemishes kept her in "the mourner's bench." She walked with bowed head. Romans 7 seemed to be her lot. She loved the Saviour with all her heart, but still Paul's cry, "Oh wretched man that I am! who shall deliver me from the body of this death?" was forever upon her lips.

The Lord led her into the experience of Romans 8 through a text in I John. It was the great crisis which marked her entrance into the promised land of a life of fulness and victory. Her Bible lay open at this text on her casket when she lay down at last to rest from her labors. One day she was reading her New Testament in the Greek as she was wont to do, when she discovered that according to the Greek, the blood of Jesus Christ, God's Son, is forever cleansing the believer who walks in the light. The verb is in the present active tense: "If we walk in the light, as he is in the light, we have fellowship one with another, and the blood of Jesus Christ his Son cleanseth [is ever cleansing] us from all sin." The result for Frances Havergal was a mighty revolution. A new day dawned. She would no longer be sad because of her faults and blemishes. She would rejoice because of the infinite efficacy of the Saviour's atoning death.

Do we not read (Rev. 12) that Michael and his angels overcame by the blood of the Lamb? There can be no victorious Christian living without this foundation. We must live hidden in the Saviour's wounds for "there is a fountain filled with blood drawn from Immanuel's veins." Any sense of guilt takes the edge off our sword. It is a short-circuit through which spiritual life escapes. We are weakened; victory slips from our grasp. So it must be the Cross every moment. Even though there be no voluntary sin, our garments are being besmirched by contact with the world.

Peter did not understand. "Lord," said he, "dost thou wash my feet?" "What I do thou knowest not now . . ." was the answer.

"Thou shalt never wash my feet," was the apostle's hot reply.

"If I wash thee not, thou hast no part with me," said the Lord.

"Lord, not my feet only, but also my hands and my head," then replies Peter.

To which the Saviour answers, "He that is washed needeth not save to wash his feet, but is clean every whit."

Our daily walk on life's dusty roads of sin, even when there is no known sin to confess, leaves its mark. How wonderful to know that all such besmirchings which contact with a world whose prince is Satan makes inevitable, even when we are wholly the Lord's, and our life is hid with Him in God, are immediately taken care of by the blood which is forever cleansing.

## Chapter XIV

## BEYOND VICTORY

There is a great beyond to victory which, if we fail to take into account, may lead us to defeat. In a sense victory is not God's ultimate. He has predestined us to be conformed to the image of His Son (Rom. 8:29). Here you have God's ultimate. Paul's supreme aspiration was that in the power of the Saviour's resurrection, and in the fellowship of His sufferings, he might be made conformable unto His death (Phil. 3:10). The victorious life which issues from a participation in the power of Christ's resurrection, as C. A Fox points out, gravitates toward the Cross. The "Lambhood" nature of Christ must be worked into the believer. In order to bring about this Christ-likeness, the Spirit of God is obligated very often to use severe measures. The Holy Spirit must apply the Cross in an ever deeper way if the believer is to be brought into full conformity to God's holy Son—the great prototype.

Bearing this in mind, we come to see that what might be looked upon as defeat is victory in its sublimest form. "To him that overcometh will I grant to sit with me in my throne, even as I also overcame, and am sat down with my Father in his throne." The Saviour overcame through the Cross. It was on Calvary that He wrought His supreme victory. In the midst of shame and ignominy and agony and death it was ever and only victory with not so much as a shadow of defeat. "Be of good cheer; I have overcome the world."

We must revise our notions of what victory really is; otherwise, we may charge up to defeat what really goes to victory. The great beyonds of victory are found in suffering for the sake of others and in seeming defeat. God does not always deliver His children from great trials and bitter losses and heart-breaking experiences of seeming defeat. The truth of the matter is that they are committed unto death for Jesus' sake that the life also of Jesus might be made manifest in their mortal flesh (II Cor. 4:11). God delivers *in* trials and losses, not *from* them. The pattern is ever the same: Golgotha. It all becomes clear; a perfect focus when we grasp the sublime fact that the Christian life springs from, and must bear the earmarks of, the uttermost tragedy of the ages. Never such a shipwreck as Calvary. To be conformed to the image of God's Son, we must be wrecked on the Rock of Ages.

Fruitfulness is another beyond of victory.

Victory has to do with my happiness alone; fruitfulness means happiness for others and is only possible through seeming defeat. The corn of wheat must fall into the ground and die, else it abideth alone, but if it die it beareth much fruit. It is in the fruit, Jesus says, that the Father is glorified. The Saviour's ultimate for His followers is much fruit—not safety, not social security, not ease, not pleasure, not prosperity. It looked like defeat when the hard-pressed apostle prayed three times that his thorn might be removed, only to receive a flat negative. "My grace is sufficient for thee." Death must work in Paul if life is to be communicated to others. This colossus of the ages who lays the foundations of a new order, the Christian dispensation, must learn to glory in the weaknesses, in persecutions, in tribulations that the power of Christ may rest upon him. He must know bitterness and death and say, "I am crucified [together] with Christ: nevertheless I live; yet not I, but Christ liveth in me ..." if God's order is to be established on earth and rivers of water of life flow out to parched, dying souls. This is victory's beyond. This *is* victory.

Henry Suso, the great German mystic, once heard a knock at his door. A strange woman stood there with a babe in her arms which she thrust into his arms, saying, "Here you have the fruit of your sin." Suso had never before seen the woman. He was as innocent as a dove. The woman hastened away leaving him with the babe. The news of what had happened went through the town like a flash. So this is the man we had revered as holy! What a hypocrite, what a fraud. Suso was crushed. He groaned like a dying man. What was he to do? He withdrew to a desert place and called upon the Lord saying it was more than he could bear. "What shall I do, Lord?" he cries in his pain and shame. "Thou knowest that I am innocent." The answer comes to him with perfect clearness and finality. "What shall you do? Do as I did; suffer for the sins of others and say nothing." Suso saw the Cross. Peace came to his troubled soul. He returned to his home; took the child and sweetly, humbly cared for the waif and reared it as if it were his very own, never saying a word in self-defense. Years later, the unknown woman returned to publish abroad Suso's innocence. But the work was done. Suso had been conformed to the image of God's Son. The beyond of victory was achieved. Here you have victory's essence, its deepest nature—"Christ in you, the hope of glory."

A sergeant of the British forces over in Egypt, manifesting a fine Christian spirit in his dealings with the men, was called before his chaplain who said, "Sergeant, tell me how you were converted." "It is very simple," replied the sergeant, "we were back at camp where we were having great sport with a Christian soldier, the only Christian in the regiment. He was the butt of jokes, jeered and mocked, and at night when he would kneel beside his cot to pray, boots would fly from every quarter aimed at his head. One night I took my boots and cracked him on the head as he knelt beside me in prayer. He said nothing. In the morning, Chaplain, I found my boots beside my bed all shined up and ready for me to get into. In this way I was paid by the one I had so cruelly wronged. Chaplain, it was too much. It broke my heart. I couldn't resist such a testimony. I surrendered to Christ."

Victory in its sublimest manifestation is nothing more nor less than the Spirit of Christ, which is love and a willingness to die for others, revealing itself under circumstances which ordinarily call forth anger, impatience, hatred and revenge. We are more than conquerors through Him that loved us.

"Love suffereth long, and is kind ... is not easily provoked ... beareth all things ... endureth all things ... Love never faileth."

## Chapter XV

## VICTORY MEANS RIGHT RELATIONS

The first requisite for a life of victory, of
course, is Christ. He must be your all in all.
For you to live must be Christ, as it was with
Paul. The second requisite is right relation-
ships with others. All turning in on self paves
the way for defeat. The eye does not turn
in on itself. It looks away from itself to its
object. The healthy soul refuses all introspec-
tion. It is not taken up with itself. It is taken
up with God and man.

Man fell when God ceased to be his center
and he shifted to self as a center. God was
driven from the throne of the heart and self
was placed upon the throne to reign. Pride
explains all the hell there is or ever will be.
Now the Christian who is fully identified with
Christ and finds in Him his all and therefore
victory, loses self and finds a universal life.
It is the life of the ages. It is the life of God.
Being a universal life, it embraces mankind.

The object of the Cross was to provide not
only remission of sins (we *do* find here our
justification), but also liberation from the
prison-house of self. "He died for all, that

they which live should not henceforth live unto themselves . . ." (II Cor. 5:15). To the degree in which "self-life" prevails, is the purpose of the Cross being frustrated.

It all comes to a clear focus in Paul's doctrine of "The body of Christ which is the church." In the body the individual member ceases to live for itself. It lives for the body. Its interests are fused with the body and its sacred Head. "For by one Spirit are we all baptized into one body . . . God hath tempered the body together . . . that there should be no schism in the body . . . Now ye are the body of Christ, and members in particular" (I Cor. 12). "Speaking the truth in love . . . grow up into him in all things, which is the head, even Christ: From whom the whole body fitly joined together and compacted by that which every joint supplieth, according to the effectual working in the measure of every part, maketh increase of the body unto the edifying of itself in love" (Eph. 4:15,16).

Now there can be no full-orbed victory without a deep recognition of the oneness of the body. Victory is enhanced to the degree in which the Christian enters into a life of communion with all true Christians regardless of name and ecclesiastical procedure and form, in a thorough-going recognition of the oneness of the body.

"When ye stand praying, forgive . . ." (Mark 11:25). Jesus had just been speaking of the authority of the believer linking it up with a spirit of forgiveness, without which the aforementioned authority is greatly weakened. If you quarrel with a brother in the faith, you weaken your tie with the body. Ill will, resentment, bitterness, unwillingness to forgive a brother who may have offended; all these are aimed at the body, and in the hour of crisis when one sorely needs the prayers of others—a sense of oneness to carry him through—they will surely come acutely to the surface and engender defeat.

God does not give the Christian victory on a basis of "aloneness," but in view of the entire body which the Holy Spirit is forming. "If two of you shall agree on earth as touching anything that they shall ask, it shall be done for them of my Father which is in heaven." The Saviour makes answered prayer hinge on oneness with a fellow-believer. To have Christ in His fullness possessing our hearts, we must be willing to receive all those whom He has redeemed and who form His body. He works through the body and any violation of this principle is disastrous in the hour of conflict. This is material for Satan to work on, and he loses no time in seizing this sort of thing and inflaming it. It is self-life in contradiction of the oneness of the body, which has an affinity with the adversary, and which God Himself respects; for He works according to law and lets Satan have what after all is his. He has power over the old creation whose basic principle is pride; but the new creation

("To make in himself of twain—Jew and Gentile—one new man . . . by the cross, having slain the enmity thereby," Eph. 2:16, 17) springs from the second Adam, the Lord Jesus Christ, and is free.

In the evil day when we are told to stand against the wiles of the Devil, we will find it a source of immeasurable strength and be more than conquerors, if we will recognize the oneness of the body and "stand in" on the prayers of all saints. This is an act of faith—the faith which "is the victory that overcometh the world." This is an Amen to what God says is true. You draw strength from the body of which you are a part. The river of water of life which proceedeth from the throne and from the Lamb, flows into the body. You cannot drink to the full if you are out of fellowship with the immediate members that link you with the body.

Now Satan may be able to stand against you and drive you from the field of battle when you have no more foundation than "selfhood"; but he can do nothing so long as the rock bottom of your being is "bodyhood." You are one with all the redeemed who make up the body of Christ, and this fact makes you invincible.

"Till we all come in the unity of the faith, and of the knowledge of the Son of God, unto a perfect man, unto the measure of the stature of the fullness of Christ" (Eph. 4:13).